Table of Contents

Can you find these words?

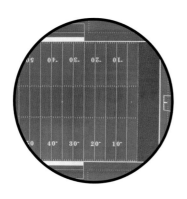

end zone

points

touchdown

uniform

Let's Play!

I play football.

uniform

I wear shoulder pads under my **uniform.**

4

I wear a helmet.

My teammate throws the ball.

I catch it. I run!

The other team tries to stop me.
I run to their **end zone**.

◄10   ◄20   ◄30   ◄40

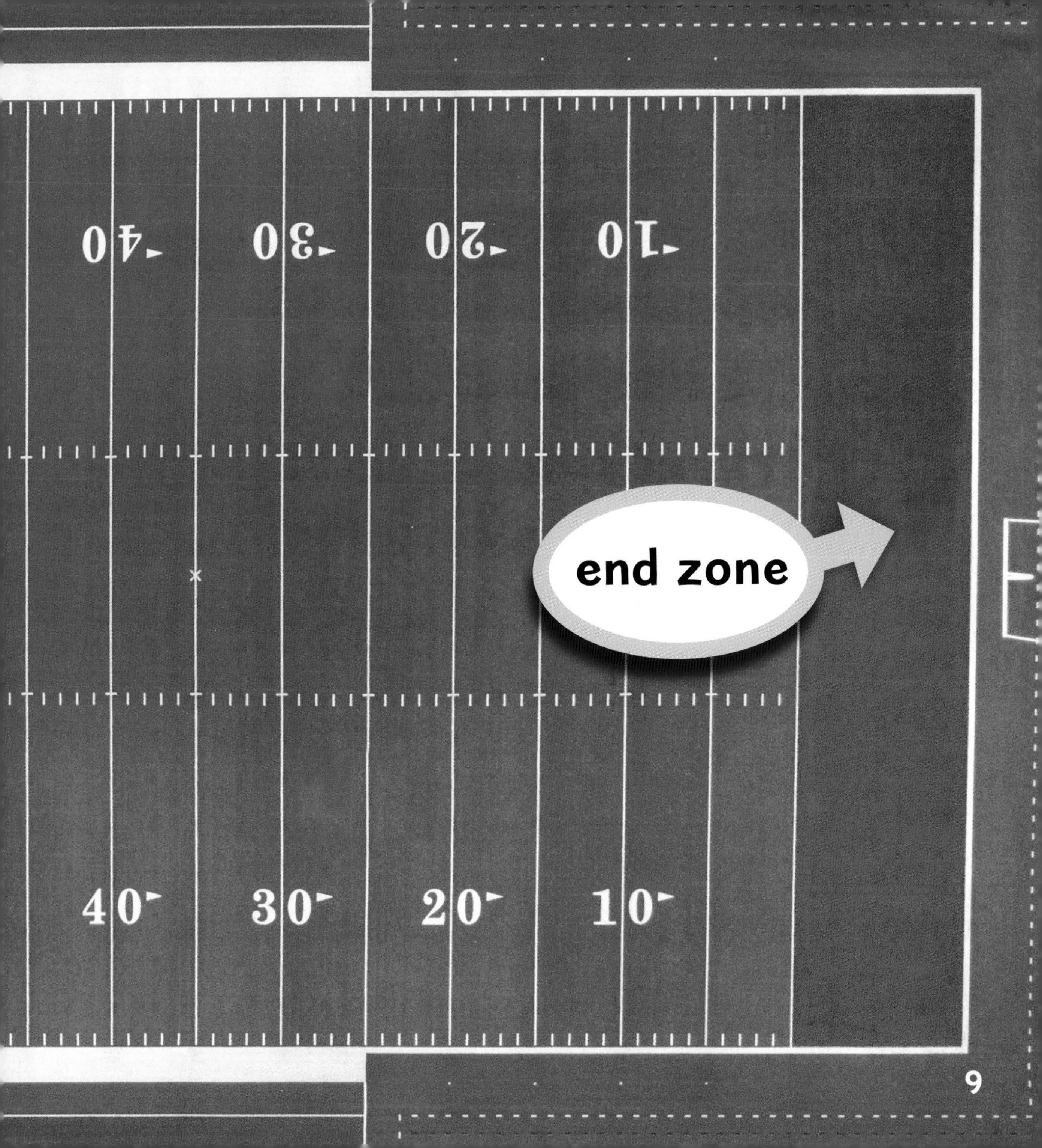
end zone
40
30
20
10

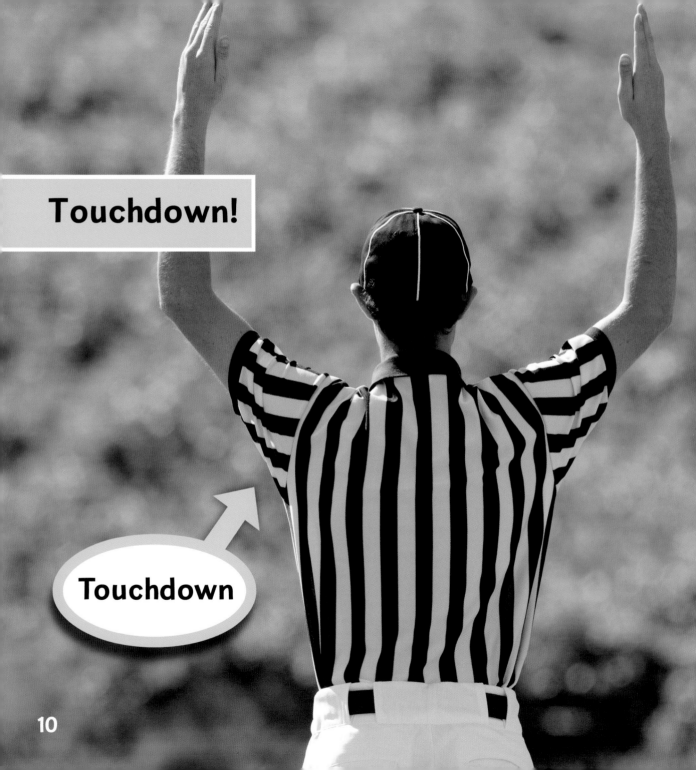

My team scores six **points**.

points

Sometimes we win.
Sometimes we lose.

We always have fun!

Did you find these words?

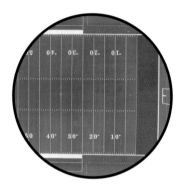

I run to their **end zone.**

My team scores six **points.**

Touchdown!

I wear shoulder pads under my **uniform.**

Photo Glossary

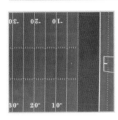 **end zone** (end zohn): The part of a football field at each end where players score points for the team.

 **points** (points): Units used for scoring in a game.

 **touchdown** (tuhch-down): In football, a play in which the ball is carried over the other team's goal line, earning six points.

 **uniform** (YOO-nuh-form): A special set of clothes worn by all the members of a team or group.

Index

About the Author

Elliot Riley is the author of dozens of books for kids. When she's not reading or writing, you can find her walking by the water in sunny Tampa, Florida.

www.rourkeeducationalmedia.com

PHOTO CREDITS: Cover: ©CatLane; p2,8,14,15: ©filo; p2,11,14,15: ©gpflman; p2,10,14,15: ©Matt_Brown; p2,3,4,14,15: ©Michael Krinke; p5: ©XiXinXing; p6: ©jonathansloane; p7: ©Andrew Rich; p12: ©Steve Debenport; p13: ©lutherhill

Edited by: Keli Sipperley
Cover by: Rhea Magaro-Wallace
Interior design by: Kathy Walsh

Library of Congress PCN Data
Football / Elliot Riley
(Ready for Sports)
ISBN 978-1-64369-054-4 (hard cover)(alk. paper)
ISBN 978-1-64369-084-1 (soft cover)
ISBN 978-1-64369-201-2 (e-Book)
Library of Congress Control Number: 2018955881

Printed in the United States of America, North Mankato, Minnesota